What Do Living Things Need?

Elizabeth Austen

Living things
need light.

Living things
need food.

Living things
need water.

Living things
need air.

Living things
need **space**.

Living things need homes.

Living things
need **protection**.

Living things need
other living things.

Let's Do Science!

What do living things need? Try this!

What to Get

- ❑ 2 paper cups
- ❑ 2 potted flowers
- ❑ soil
- ❑ water

What to Do

1. Plant the flowers in the cups. Put them in a sunny place.

2. Water one cup each day. Do not water the other cup.

3. After a few days, what do you see? Is there a difference between the flowers?

Glossary

protection—a thing that keeps something safe

space—an empty area

Index

Your Turn!

Look at some plants. What plants have everything they need? What plants do not? How can you tell?

Consultants

Sally Creel, Ed.D.
Curriculum Consultant

Leann Iacuone, M.A.T., NBCT, ATC
Riverside Unified School District

Jill Tobin
California Teacher of the Year
Semi-Finalist
Burbank Unified School District

Publishing Credits

Conni Medina, M.A.Ed., *Managing Editor*
Lee Aucoin, *Creative Director*
Diana Kenney, M.A.Ed., NBCT, *Senior Editor*
Lynette Tanner, *Editor*
Lexa Hoang, *Designer*
Hillary Dunlap, *Photo Editor*
Rachelle Cracchiolo, M.S.Ed., *Publisher*

Image Credits: pp.18–19 (illustrations) Rusty Kinnunen; all other images from Shutterstock.

Library of Congress Cataloging-in-Publication Data

Austen, Elizabeth (Elizabeth Charlotte), author.
What do living things need? / Elizabeth Austen.
pages cm
Summary: "It is time to learn what life needs."—Provided by publisher.
Audience: K to grade 3.
Index.
ISBN 978-1-4807-4523-0 (pbk.) —
ISBN 978-1-4807-5132-3 (ebook)
1. Life (Biology—Juvenile literature.
2. Readers (Primary) I. Title.
QH309.2.A972 2015
570—dc23
2014008921

Teacher Created Materials
5301 Oceanus Drive
Huntington Beach, CA 92649-1030
http://www.tcmpub.com

ISBN 978-1-4807-4523-0

Printed by: 51497
Printed in: China